# THE NUTCRACKER

Arranged by Chad Johnson

T0081565

ISBN 978-1-4803-4553-9

HAL•LEONARD®
CORPORATION

7777 W. BLUEMOUND RD. P.O. BOX 13819 MILWAUKEE, WI 53213

In Australia Contact:
**Hal Leonard Australia Pty. Ltd.**
4 Lentara Court
Cheltenham, Victoria, 3192 Australia
Email: ausadmin@halleonard.com.au

For all works contained herein:
Unauthorized copying, arranging, adapting, recording, Internet posting, public performance,
or other distribution of the printed music in this publication is an infringement of copyright.
Infringers are liable under the law.

Visit Hal Leonard Online at
**www.halleonard.com**

# Overture

By Pyotr Il'yich Tchaikovsky

Copyright © 2013 by HAL LEONARD CORPORATION
International Copyright Secured   All Rights Reserved

3

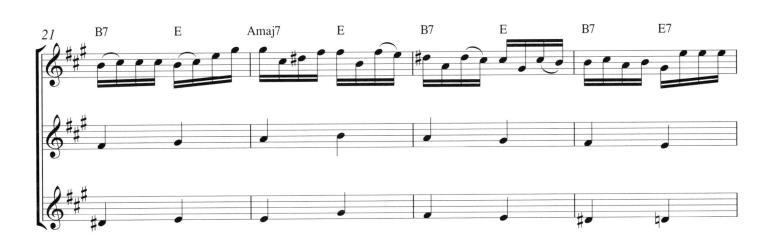

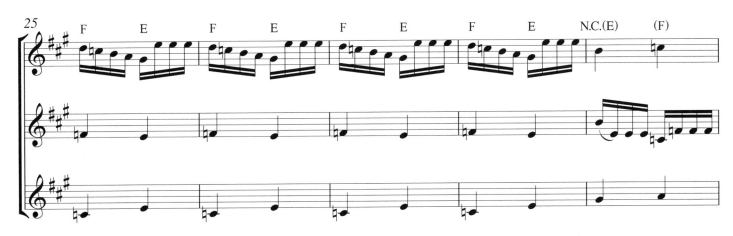

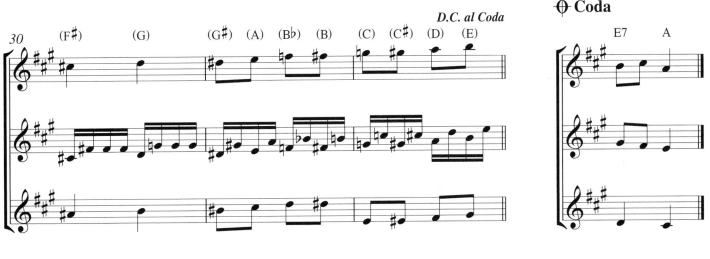

# March

By Pyotr Il'yich Tchaikovsky

Copyright © 2013 by HAL LEONARD CORPORATION
International Copyright Secured   All Rights Reserved

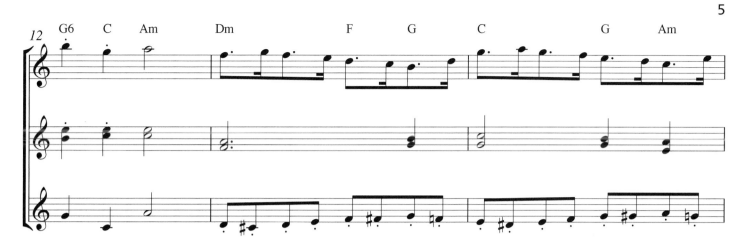

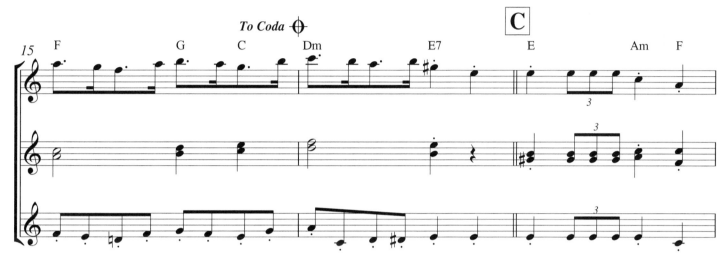

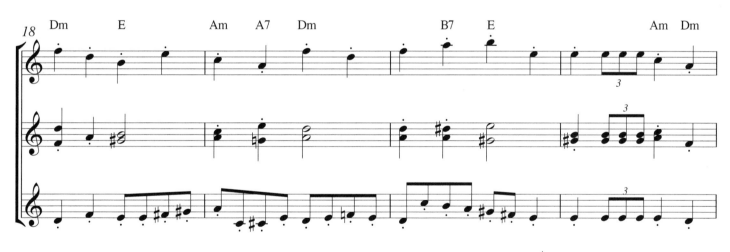

# Dance of the Sugar Plum Fairy

By Pyotr Il'yich Tchaikovsky

Copyright © 2013 by HAL LEONARD CORPORATION
International Copyright Secured   All Rights Reserved

**D**

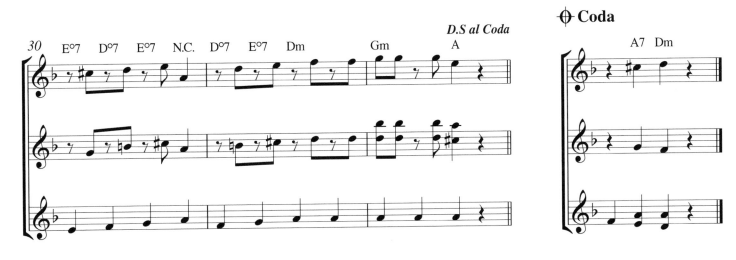

# Russian Dance
## ("Trepak")
By Pyotr Il'yich Tchaikovsky

Copyright © 2013 by HAL LEONARD CORPORATION
International Copyright Secured   All Rights Reserved

# Arabian Dance
## ("Coffee")

By Pyotr Il'yich Tchaikovsky

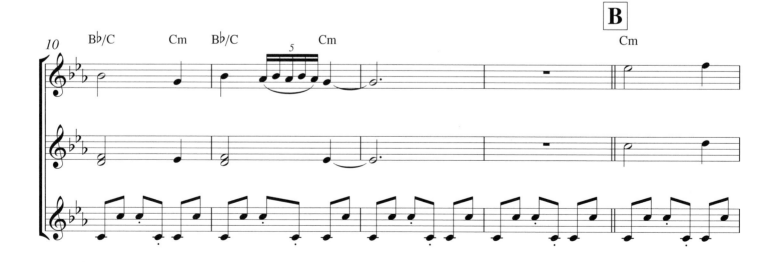

Copyright © 2013 by HAL LEONARD CORPORATION
International Copyright Secured   All Rights Reserved

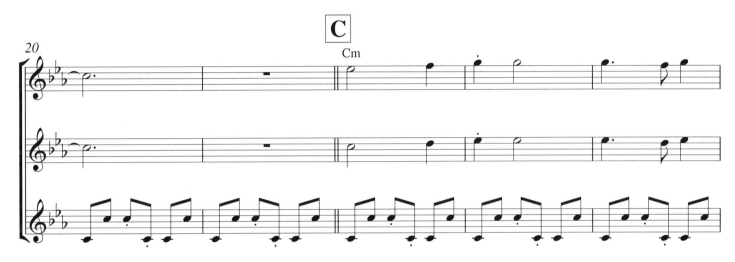

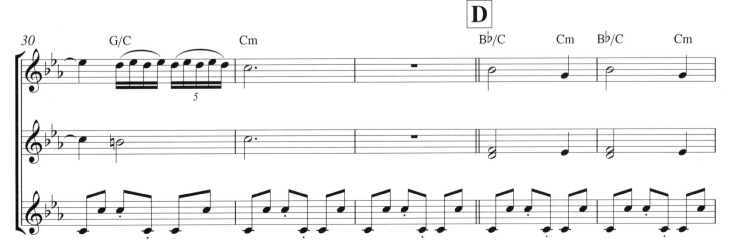

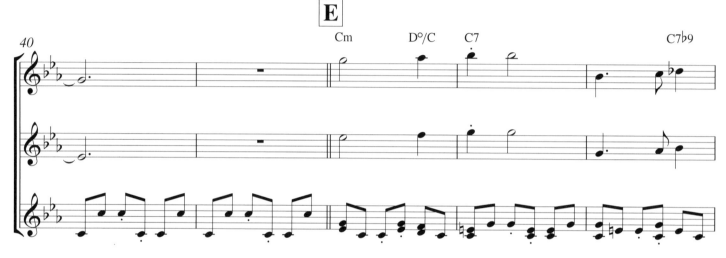

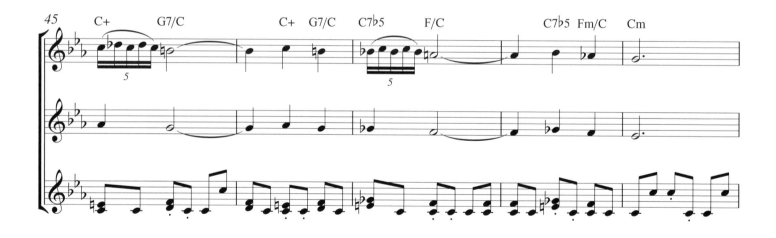

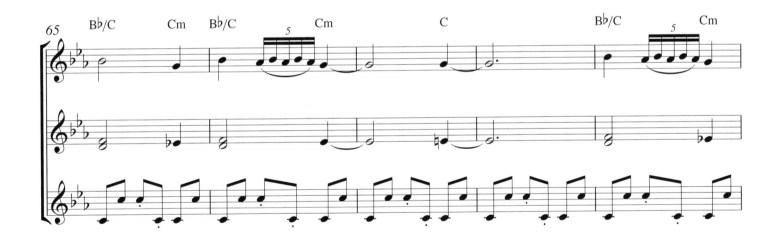

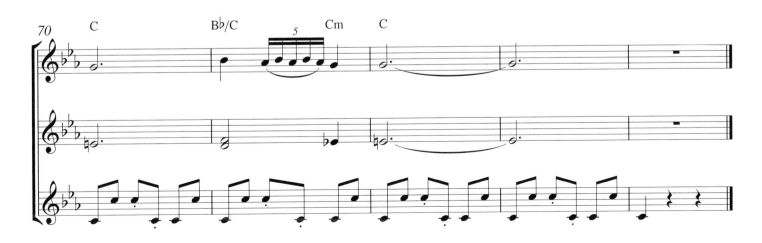

# Chinese Dance
## ("Tea")

By Pyotr Il'yich Tchaikovsky

Copyright © 2013 by HAL LEONARD CORPORATION
International Copyright Secured   All Rights Reserved

**B**

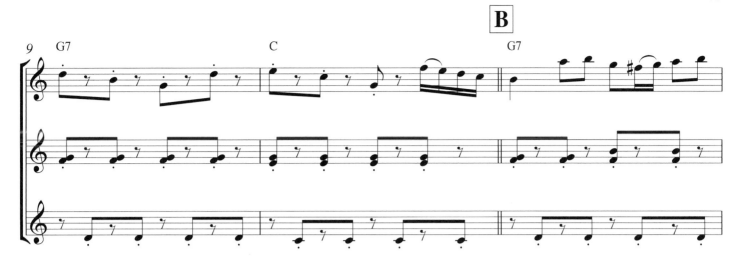

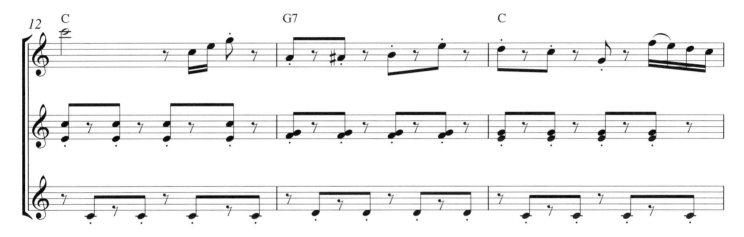

**C**

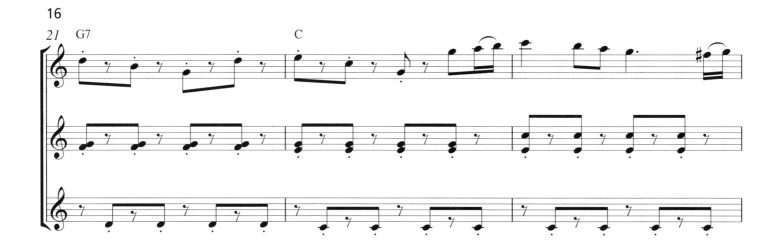

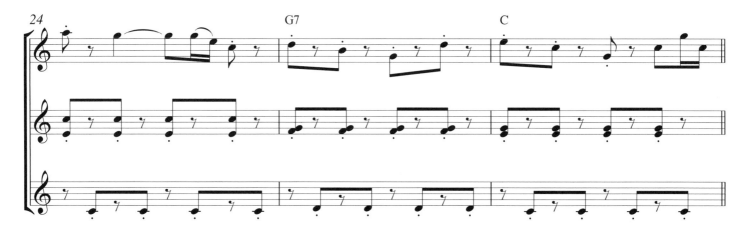

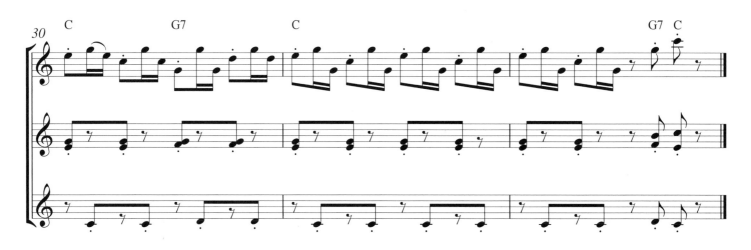

This page has been intentionally left blank.

# Dance of the Reed-Flutes

By Pyotr Il'yich Tchaikovsky

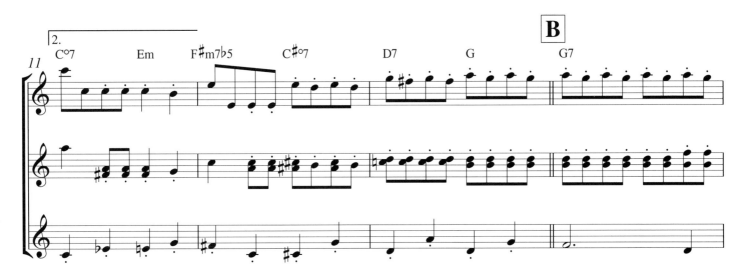

Copyright © 2013 by HAL LEONARD CORPORATION
International Copyright Secured   All Rights Reserved

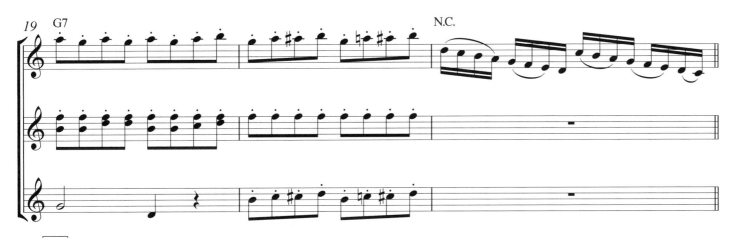

# Waltz of the Flowers

By Pyotr Il'yich Tchaikovsky

Copyright © 2013 by HAL LEONARD CORPORATION
International Copyright Secured   All Rights Reserved

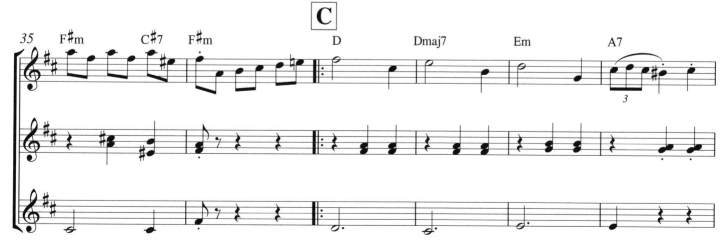

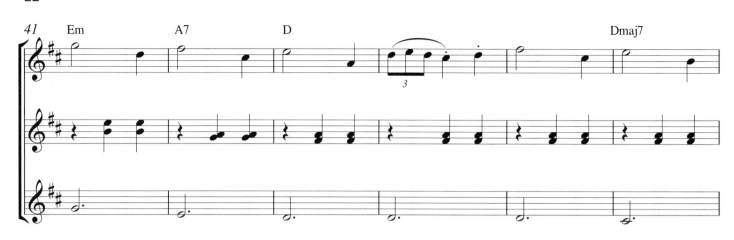

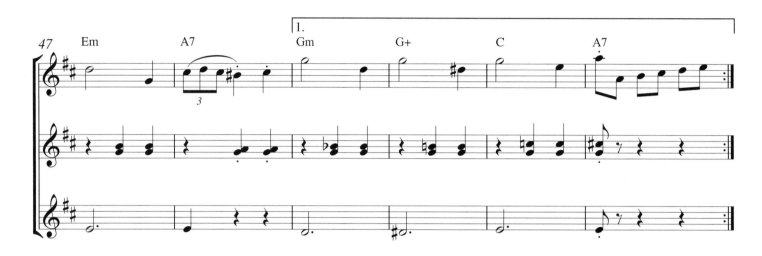

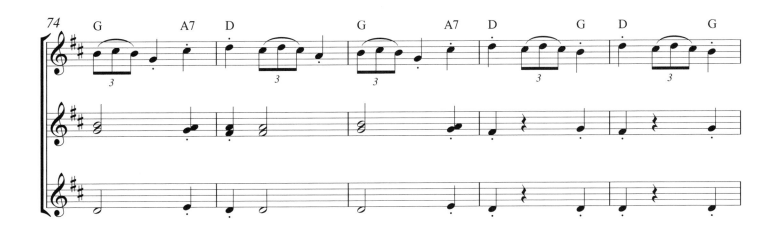

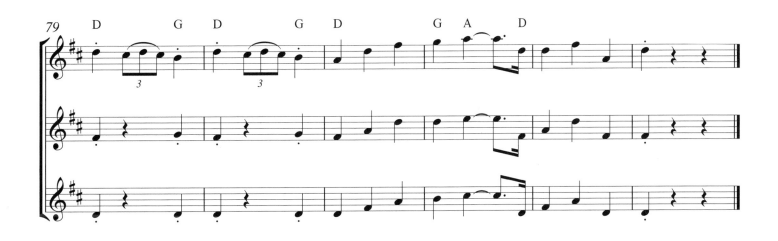

## NOTES FROM THE ARRANGER

Arranging for three ukuleles can be challenging because of the instrument's limited range. In standard tuning (G-C-E-A), there is only one octave plus a major sixth between the open C string and fret 12 on the A string. Certain melodies easily span this distance and more, so compromises sometimes had to be made.

Not all ukuleles have the same number of frets. If your uke has fewer than 15 frets, you may need to play certain phrases an octave lower (especially in Part I). Some phrases have already been transposed up or down an octave—this was only done out of necessity and kept to a minimum. A few songs require every inch of available fretboard, but fret 15 on the first string (high C) is the limit, and this is extremely rare.

The three voices will sometimes cross as a result of range limitations. If Part III is considered to be the "bass" line, keep in mind that the lowest available "bass" notes are sometimes on the first string! However, if you own a baritone ukulele, almost all of the notes in Part III could be played an octave lower (except the open C string and C♯ on fret 1), thus providing a more effective bass line.

Despite the above caveats, I believe that the spirit of these songs has been preserved, and I hope you enjoy playing these arrangements as much as I enjoyed creating them. By the way, a fourth ensemble part can be added by strumming along with the chord symbols!

– Chad Johnson

## SOPRANO, CONCERT & TENOR FRETBOARD

## BARITONE FRETBOARD

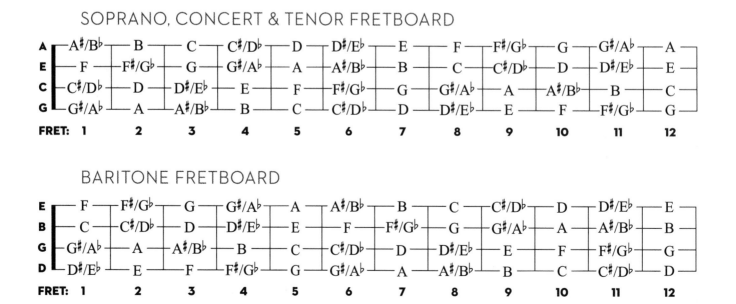